C000094670

COLLE

POETRY

Para a minha querida Mariana, um beijo londrino muito especial!

[signature]

26 Nov 2011

Chiado Publishing

chiadopublishing.com

All characters and events in this publication, other than those
clearly in the public domain, are ficticious and any resemblance to
real persons, living or dead, is purely coincidential.

chiadopublishing.com

Copyright © 2011 by Chiado Publishing and Paulo M. Franco
All rights reserved.

Published by:
Chiado Publishing
Break Media Holding

Rua do Açúcar, n.º 86
1950-010 Lisboa
PORTUGAL

Porte de Paris
50 Avenue du President Wilson Bâtiment 112
La Plaine St Denis 93214
FRANCE

Internet: www.chiadopublishing.com | www.chiadoglobal.com
For international orders please visit: www.chiadopublishing.com

Title: Beyond my self – A collection of 80 poems on Life
Author: Paulo M. Franco

Graphic Design: José S. Peixoto – Chiado Publishing

Printed and Bound by: BREAK PRINT

ISBN: 978-989-697-293-6
Legal Deposit n.º 332187/11

PAULO M. FRANCO

Beyond my self

A collection of 80 poems on Life

Chiado Publishing

"The supreme good is like water, which nourishes all things without trying to. It flows to low places loathed by all men.Therefore, it is like the Tao.

Live in accordance with the nature of things. In dwelling, be close to the land. In meditation, go deep in the heart. In dealing with others, be gentle and kind. Stand by your word. Govern with equity. Be timely in choosing the right moment.

One who lives in accordance with nature does not go against the way of things. He moves in harmony with the present moment, always knowing the truth of just what to do."

Lao-tzu

"To enjoy good health, to bring true happiness to one's family, to bring peace to all, one must first discipline and control one's own mind. If a man can control his mind he can find the way to Enlightenment, and all wisdom and virtue will naturally come to him."

Gautama Buddha

"Your vision will become clear only when you look into your heart. Who looks outside, dreams. Who looks inside, awakens."

Carl Gustav Jung

Index

Preface

When I first read Paulo M. Franco's poems, one of the first things that came straight to my mind was the following: "Why in English?" Interestingly enough, this is one of the few questions which are not explicitly addressed in the Afterword which the author was careful enough to add at the end of his compilation of eighty poems.

The truth is that the author is someone who has the Portuguese citizenship and who, although having a bachelor degree in English Studies, is not quite bilingual – which deepens the mystery around the fluency in which he writes poetry in English. Or, by quoting his own words, the fluency with which the poetic writing in English happens to him.

The chronological sequence of the poems, which begins with the date January, 12th 1998 and ends on November, 1st 2010, encompassing, in this way, a period of twelve years, allows us to go along the most persistent isotopies in his lyrical speech and, at the same time, to spot the semantic and formal variations that appear along the path. In what concerns the most significant image and lexical pattern in the group of poems, the echoes and resonances of the English Romantic poetry, mostly William Wordsworth's, are the ones which, in my opinion, come apart from the whole, even though they concentrate themselves, in a more stressed way, in the less recent poems.

Words and expressions such as "past glories", "glimpses", "moments past", "the innocence of the child", "the inner voice", "ages lost", "splendour", "eternal bliss", "joyful bliss", "visionaries", "shadows", "contemplation", "dreaming", evoke a poetic language and a neoplatonic conception of the Universe very similar to the ones we find, for example, in Wordsworth's "Immortality Ode", also reminding us of the pre-romantic William Blake's *Songs of Innocence*. The meditative contemplation of human life associated to images of Nature, the notion of the pre-existence of the soul and its immortality, moulded in the typical childhood reminiscences and of the states of innocence, run through Paulo M. Franco's poems, being their deepest semantic and imagistic structure.

On the other hand, mainly in more recent poems, that dialogic relationship with a poetic speech eminently romantic intertwines with terms and concepts from other sources and traditions, such is the case of the karmic matrix from the Buddhist and Hindu thought, or the phenomenon of synchronicity such as it was analysed by the 20th century psychologist Carl Jung.

In short, it is about the interlacing of the currents of thought which, from the East to the West and along the centuries, have built a view on the Universe, which does not abdicate from the idea of Transcendency, receiving it, instead, as the spiritual origin of all meaning, independently from the fact of its being intelligible or not.

In Paulo M. Franco's poems that view is underlying not only to those which adopt a more intimate thematic, addressing feelings, emotions and human relationships, but also to those who, in the context of a metalanguage, question the sense of art and the act itself of writing poetry. That is the case of the poems entitled "Declaration of Intentions", "The Notion of Poetry", "The Quest for Art", "Unlimited Art" and "Void".

Resuming the notion of a process whose genesis belongs to the realms of the unconscious, poetry defines itself as something which imposes itself to the subject of enunciation, operating through it – let us remind ourselves of the author's words in the Afterword: "Why writing happens through me". That is to say, it is up to the poet the psychic function of verbalizing the perplexities, the interrogations and the answers, the doubts and the certainties, which might arise from an attentive eye around him, as well as from another dimension, perhaps with an archetypical profile, in consonance with the platonic perspective, and much more real than the one we usually call "reality".

I can only add that all of this manifests itself in a way of expression composed by a language rich in images and metaphors of a great sensitivity, besides having a cadence, a rhythm and a musicality which grant it an enchanting power – a power which, ultimately, sends us back to Plato, especially to the dialogue entitled *Ion*, where he stresses the idea of the divine origin of poetic inspiration.

Maria Isabel Barbudo, PhD
(Professor of English Literature
Head of the English Department
University of Lisbon, Portugal)

Enduring

Today we have endured
Another day
Another time
Another fight.

Tomorrow is uncertainty.
It can only be envisioned
Through the veils of mystery
Of Fate, of one's karma.
To dare is the utmost
Challenge
It is the very essence
Dreams are made of.

Not to dare
Is to die
Is not taking part
In Life's greatest symphony
The Absolute attempt
To produce something
Out of nowhere
To achieve
What cannot be achieved
Without striving:
Life!

12/01/98

The eyes of people

The eyes of people
Are filled with despair
Disillusion
Hopelessness
Vanquished by another day
Thrown at the edge of a dream
In the nightmare of existence.

The power of the unknown
Cries on the virtues
Of the unseen, the untouched
And the unspoken.

The virtue of life
Is brought about
By heroic moments,
Spared by someone,
Trying to survive,
Trying not to drown.

The silence that emerges
Cannot be heard
Only felt, touched
On somebody's heart...

12/01/98

Bold and daring

Bold and daring
Facing each day
The challenges of dismay
Collapsing
One after the other
Pretending
What was never seen
Hoping for the goal to achieve
Wanting
For the love to have lived.

13/01/98

Whatever

Whatever the colours may be
I will be here for you
Whatever the feelings you may feel
I will be one with you
Whatever the wishes you may have
I will understand you
Whatever reactions you may find
I will be your safe haven

Because when you see
I am in your eyes
When you feel
I am in your heart
When you wish
I wish for us both
When you face challenges
I am always by your side.

14/05/00

Shadows

There are shadows
That lie beneath
The surface
Of one's being

There are cries
That echo
Through realms
Of past glories

There are people
Who stumble
In the darkness
Of their consciousness...

Yet I foresee
The glimpses of tomorrow
The beacons of illumination
Breaking down the shackles
Of torment
Of suffering
Of pain...

It is yet
To come
It is bound
To happen
But when?

24/10/00

Challenges

There are many ways
But only one Path.
The true nature of the Self
Longs for the gathering
For the Oneness of attainment.
Yet the Path has many distractions
And each passing moment
It gets further and further away...

Suddenly, the true Self,
Always present, always listening
Makes way for the feeling to occur
For a word of wisdom
To resound
From the deepest layer
Of Being,
Awakening the soul
To the Path of enlightenment
Through self knowledge
To meditation
On Life itself,
On the true nature of things,
Of the core and meaning of the Truth.

I long to enter the waves
Of Cosmos and of the Essence...

29/11/00

Unspoken

Doubtless of moments past
Thine are the certainties
Of time and place
Of wonders unveiled and shown
Before the very eyes of people
To be seen and to be heard
In each beautiful passing moment
To be grasped and tasted
With patience and utmost care
To experience the mystery of Life
In every step of the Path
In every walk of Life
Thou are there
Unseen, unheard, untouchable
But so present
In your presence.

Unspoken are the words
Uttered by the earth, the sea and the wind...

29/11/00

Madness

A state of mind
A way of being
Happy or sad?
Not knowing
Or knowing too much?
Unaware
Or too much aware
Of the nature of things?
Disturbed
Disturbing...

How can we ignore them?
We can't
They have already
Ignored themselves...
They leave us
Powerless
In the presence
Of their unpresence.
Are they there?
Is there a person
Dwelling?

Internal winds blow
Mixing and confusing
Ideas, thoughts,
Feelings and words,
Disturbing the Self
And then,
Reflections appear
In the form
Of shadows

Mumbling of words
Trembling of limbs
A distorted figure
Uncertain
About each passing day
Unwilling
To return
From nowhere...

30/11/00

The days are not the same

The days are not the same
You and I are not the same
Nothing stays the same...
Change is upon us all
And nothing is left unaffected...

Are we still here
Or are we dreaming we are?
Gazing at Life
In search for its meaning
In every passing moment
In moments of tranquillity
Brought about by contemplation
Patient and serene
The simplicity of the essence
That lies obvious and shouting
To be heard and seen
Grasped by the inner sense
The innocence of the child
Unquestioned
Untouched
For that is the Truth
Wherever we stand
Whatever we stare at
It is there
Waiting for the right moment
To be unlocked, released
Vigourlessly
Effortlessly
Every step of the Way
Following the Path
Letting itself go

Without wanting
Nor wishing
But going, going forth
Again and again
Until that moment
That bit of Wholeness
Of certainty
Given by no law
No reasoning
No logic
But to feel
Deep
To the inner core
Of Being
Of achievement
Without conscious intent
Without knowing for sure
Unless there is letting go
Into the realms of dreams
Of the motion of the ocean
Wavelike movement
Of the soul
Each moment is never the same...

13/12/00

To be...

To be or not to be
Is that really the question?
To feel or not to feel
Is it not a necessity?
To dare or not to dare
Is it not vital?
To admit or not to admit
Is it not essential?
To understand or not to understand
Is it not our goal?

For it is in being
That we discover who we are
It is in feeling
That we develop our senses
It is in daring
That we overcome challenges
It is in admitting
That we realize the truth
It is in understanding
That we truly find the essence of Life.

23/12/01

Sudden clash

Once upon a moment
You enter my room
Wishing to communicate
Silence is ready to be broken
Yet, words don't flow freely
And distance haunts
The gathering of worlds
Too far apart.

You look at me
And, in between,
Nothing flows out
From my mouth
And I imagine and wish for
The longing of good days past...

27/05/02

Indecision

Not knowing what to do
Nor how to do it
Leads us towards
Our very existence:
We are passers-by
In Life,
We are not really a part of it.

Indecisions, anguish,
Daydreaming, lack of self-esteem,
All deviate us from the core
Of perception and of living.

There is no way out
Only a way into ourselves
Because we must do
What we must do
And each one must obey
The inner voice, the inner calling,
Heard in the middle of
No sound, of complete silence,
For there will be an answer
To our longing
For wholeness,
Oneness of intent...

Beauty, Truth and Peace
Arise from that moment on
And a flash, a fragment
Of time and place
Will be ours
To help enduring the passing of days...

27/05/02

Freedom

Freedom is not a state
It is a way of being
Belonging to a higher degree
Of achievement
And of awareness.

One does belong
To a frame of ideals
Making a stand
In time and place
Being unique and only
It takes is a gentle touch
Of the soul
Coming forth from within
Like a sweet yet steady breeze
Affecting the world
With its own pace
Achieving greatness
And surmountable deeds
In moments of peril
In places of danger
The collective gathering
Of determined individuals
Make the difference
And a gigantic tidal wave
Sweeps away dictators
And entire systems
Crumble down
Leaving nothing but mere traces
To remind Humankind
How fragile and delicate
Freedom is...

14/06/02

You are

Beyond and behind you
There is a shadow
That lies beneath
Your very eyes
Eyes filled with fear
Deception
And then
The one you see
Forgets who he really is
Prevented from knowing
Where he stands
Doing unexpected things
And walking down corridors
That lead to nowhere.

You are there
Nothing else shows
But you
Wearing a smile
And wanting
For the truth to be achieved
Oh yes, you are there
But nobody listens to you
Nobody cares who you are
What you do
In the deception you create
All around you
And no one seems to care
Or to notice you...

You are what you are
You are what you see

You are who you trust
You are who you find
At the end of the corridor
There are shadows
That lie in front of you
And dim away
While you are there
Not wanting to be seen
Not wanting to be heard
Unnoticed you are
Uncared
Untouched
Untouchable
And yet
You foresee the future
That fate has reserved
For you
You are
You see
No one
But you
Undisputedly
Undoubtedly
You are
You.

31/10/03

The blind man

The blind man passes
Chanting his plaintive song
Asking for a mere coin.
People look aside
Indifferent to his passing
And days roll on and on
The same sounds,
The same faces,
Face him but don't care
At all.

He's there, I'm here
And each has a calling,
A reason for being here
Passing by, frequently,
Unaware of the others
And of their needs
Or wishes, or dreams.

We are moving
Can't stop now
Must hurry
No time to waste
For anyone
Not in the least
For him.
Who cares?
The blind man passes
Unheard and unnoticed...

05/06/04

The art of living

The art of living
Is the way we live our lives
Standing on a fiery rock
Facing the world beneath
Dealing with memories
Of moments past
Trying to recall the ages lost
And pretending not to see
The obviousness of the truths
Within.

The anchor of satisfaction
Closes its eyes to remembrance
And changes the notion
Of oblivion, despair and infatuation
Guided in the twilight
Wanting to find an answer
Never wishing to transform
But to absorb reality.

Dreams are meant to be
Lived in a crazy symphony
Depending on the time and place
Never ceasing to flow into eternity.

Changes occur
Dreams are fulfilled
And the both of us
Become intertwined
As one, as two
Together in oneness
In silence

In awe
Commemorating the vastness
Of the ocean
And of our essence
Lost but finally found
As we encounter that point
Of unity, communion of soul
Oblivious of the worldly pleasures
And illusions
We are – One
Forever
As the world is one
But unnoticed
Unpromised
And daring to find
The way
Into us all
Into our belonging
Together, forever.

The age of time
Has come to pass
And united we are
And will be
Don't you agree?

07/06/04

Man versus Woman

A man has got to do
What a man has got to do.
And a woman?
A woman has got to do
Even more!

Celebrate your humankind
Or celebrate your womankind?
She is where we come from
She is who we go to
Looking for protection
Looking for love
Looking for everything
Looking for who we are.

Finding our source
Finding our missing half
Looking ahead
One with each other
Parallel paths
Joint efforts
Strong bonds
Even if invisible
But there
Always.

What must we prove?
That we are different
But the same
Under the deep blue sky.
Even. Forever.

16/06/04

Puzzlement

Her face hides mysteries
Of things unheard
And she stands
Close to everybody else
But detached from the world
Seeming to drift away
In the midst of melancholic mist
Present but fading away
Before my eyes.

Yet, she keeps coming back,
The same posture,
The same sad eyes,
Wandering thoughts
Trying to solve
The mystery of her life,
Without succeeding.

And she keeps staring
At the void,
Directly into the emptiness
Of her bewilderment,
Unaware of others,
Unconscious of herself,
Alone in the middle of so many...

22/6/04

Absolute love

She spoke of love,
He spoke of flowers.
She spoke of commitment,
He spoke of rivers.

In between, differences,
In expectations, a two-fold path,
And in dreams, untouchable.

Still converging,
Still united
By uncommon bonds,
Adapting, adjusting behaviours
In a quest for self-reliance
And the survival of each self,
Centred in priorities
And individual needs.

To compromise,
To adapt, in search for consensus
And for common grounds,
Each one driven away
By different tides of Life,
Leading them astray…

28/06/04

Jasmine Drops

A mixture of scents
Floating in the air
Fills my heart
With soothing feelings
And wraps my being
Drenched in love.

Sensing your being
Experiencing the utmost
Feelings together
Within each other
And we arrive
To a stand still
Suspended in timeless
Fragments of moments
Inspired by fragrances
Blown through an atmosphere
Rich in spices, sweet
And smooth candle lights
Intensify each aspect
Of ourselves and long
For the yearning
To be bonded
But inevitably free
Like a boundless wind
Through fields
Of green and blue...

26/10/04

Introspection

Come and sit
Next to me.
Close your eyes
And breathe deeply.
In a moment
You find yourself
Deepening your senses,
Awakening to soft
And peaceful sensations,
Seeming to drift away
Into the realm of dreams,
Where anything is possible
And reality is but a mere
Remembrance of so many *déjà vus*.

Keep going, keep letting yourself flow
In a downward spiral towards your core
Of being, here and there and everywhere,
Whoever you are, wherever you reach,
All is right, all is won and acquired
By your infinite capacity to behold
And absorb, melting into the vastness
Of wholeness, becoming and achieving a state
Of profound bliss and communion with all Creation.

In a moment, you will be
Coming back to physical reality,
Slowly and patiently,
While you adapt
To the thickening
Of normality,
Yet keeping the notion

And the memory
Of selfless realization.

28/10/04

Realization

Is experience wrong?
Is disillusion right?
The quest for the senses
Is futile because limited,
Vague and ephemeral,
Always wanting to achieve
Something that is beyond
The true nature of being.

Sensations come and go,
Feelings drift away in the dark
Side corners of the Self,
Always pressing to attain more
And more is never enough
For it always ends and ceases
To exist except in the memory,
The sanctuary of experience
Where huge amounts of moments
Are recorded and stored away,
Only accessed in bits and pieces,
Shreds of life in motion
And the notion of precariousness
Disturbs the Self away
From inner visions, glimpses
Of Eternity, escaping through
The fingers of the will to endure
One more time, again and again,
Until one realizes that all is illusion
And Reality cannot be perceived
Except by the inner sense,
In the deep silence of the soul.

Second thoughts? Always.
Certainties? Never...

26/11/04

Depression

Among the mist and the shadows
Within the disturbed mind,
Facing the brightness of Life
With gloomy and dimmed eyes,
Dragging the Self along the way,
Feeling battered and helpless,
Unable to raise the heart
Towards the self-restricted light,
A formless being crawls
Underneath the surface of emotional sanity
Sinking relentlessly in a downward drift,
An inevitable wreck on the shores of Life.

Behind curtains shut from the inside
An entity dwells in solitude,
Unable to react before daily happenings,
Envisioning them as tremendous challenges
That bend and bind the self-esteem away,
Motionlessness dominates each step not taken,
And permeates the atmosphere
With coldness and distant feelings,
Preventing all action from occurring,
Caused by an inevitable status of despair,
Petals dropping from a withered flower,
Vanquished without a struggle.

30/11/04

Magnitude

Once you decide
There is no turning back.

And why would I want
To turn my back to the future?
I have made up my mind
I am departing towards opportunity.

Beware of the dangers hidden
Disguised as promises of pleasure
Wealth and grandeur
Set out to distract and distort
Pureness of intent,
Corrupting bodies and souls alike.

Not to worry
I have had a glimpse
Of the path ahead
And I have read
Wise words of sage men of old
Who have instructed my steps and deeds
To accept and to understand
All that may come my way.
And thus, shielded in humble wisdom
The road ahead is ready
For the taking and for acceptance.

And do you think
There will be no surprises?

No, I do long for them
As opportunities

To put my spirit to the test
To let my inside being decide
Wisely and surely
On every occasion and event
What to say and what to do
And then, what must happen
Will come to pass
For only fools believe in coincidence
By chance and not by fate.

Are you ready?

Yes, indeed I am.
I am ready to experience Life!

19/12/04

Yonder Love

True love is but a shadow
Of what you have tasted
Senseless and weary of all
That disturbs the mind
By a certain grasp of reality
Or of another illusion
Brought about by your faith,
Your reckless stupor wandering
In the dark, which envisions
And catches a mere glimpse
Of a certainty that cannot be hidden.

Oh well, for yours is the splendour
And the vigour of yonder heights
Delights my very being, awakens feelings
And senses I knew not I had,
And dies by the shore of your body,
Your mind, your heart and yet
That doesn't forsake me completely,
It only dashes to and fro
In the abyss of my great wonder,
Half lost in an unknown and vague world
Beneath the great blue sky
And the dark grey clouds,
Tension builds up, like a violin string,
Ready for chanting a symphony or a duet,
Chasing a madman's dream,
Unsure and unaware of all events,
It is blown away into nothingness,
Pale and weak, you fail to weep,
Incapable of reacting or responding
To such frail but obvious intent,

Seemingly lost and chasing nothing
Of what it seemed to be...

Farewell, dear love, farewell
Until we unite again, one day...

27/04/05

Smoking Life Away

Gone into the world
From old ages past
You have conquered followers
Attracted by your insidious nature
And your dominating charm.
You convert them by the millions
Who become tied by your convincing attraction
Never letting any one go away easily
Because you disguise and confuse
Pleasure with pain,
Satisfaction with nervousness,
If they dare to live without you.

Your mysterious controlling essence
Demands always more
And it is only when challenged
That you reveal your true self,
Horrendous, demon-like face
And you enwrap your victim like a snake,
Pressing and squeezing the body and mind
Causing pain and a feeling of emptiness,
Convincing your prey that there is no life
Without your ever present influence.

Despite all campaigns to prevent your spread
You are like a plague
Attracting young fragile minds
Towards your luring personality
Convincing them into your midst
Conveying images of success and attainment in life
Persuading even the most brilliant minds
That it not worth living away from you.

But one day
Your reign will come to an end
You will be cornered without escape
Rejected and looked down upon
And mankind will surely, truly know
How to disregard you for good.

22/07/05

Suicide

There are pains that cannot be borne,
There are people who bear indescribable burdens
From within, that cannot be seen
Nor measured, only felt
And to the rest of the world
It is incomprehensible,
Out of reach, beyond any logic.

But what is logic?
What are the patterns of normality?
Who is sane and who isn't?
The ones who see too much
Or the ones that are joyfully blind?

The soul within must deal with much
And the temperament isn't always swift.
We must bear witness to our own existence
And be accountable for it,
Even if the road is too sinuous or bumpy.

We are all alone, when it comes
To the matters of the mind and heart
And what I feel cannot be felt
By anybody else, in the same way or measure,
Neither what I suffer or rejoice for
Can be understood
By the noisy and disturbing outside world.

Therefore, judging others should not be done
By any means or ways, when individuals
Take dire, pain-inflicting decisions on themselves.
Are they lucid? Do they know the path

They will be walking?
Is it a conscious, oriented decision?
Or is it merely a last resort escape,
To depart and cut themselves from
The excruciating agony of inner pain?
But then, there is no turning back,
No repentance is possible nor available anymore
And what once was, is no more.

And how does one deal with such a loss?
Life flows in mysterious ways
And trying to embrace it all at once
Is simply not possible to grasp
By the human mind alone,
Too narrow to perceive the vastness of the Spirit
And the endless opportunities it conveys.

Life is too sacred to be wasted
In purposeless ways.
Choose Life, not denial,
For it is too precious to be forsaken.

6/06/05

Declaration of intentions

I take my poetry
Very seriously.
How could I not
If it tries to mirror
My own perception
Of Life?

Dimmed as they may be
My senses try to absorb
And filter the intricacy
That makes the web of Life.

Sometimes nearsighted
I experience outside events
From within
Reflecting upon the nature of things
Determined to unveil the meaning
And the causes behind and beyond
The course of events
The unfolding of situations...

And so I go along a path
Speculating about what I see
What I perceive inside
As waves of shock striking me
Sometimes violently
Some other times softly
But always leaving traces...

And so I try to cope
With the magnitude of an infinite
Permanent wondering attitude

Not being able to choose
Whether to write or not
But aspiring to quench the thirst
In the fountain of wisdom
And self-knowledge...

25/10/05 – 30/08/09

Proving a Point

Surprises surmount expectations
When one is not ready
For what was supposed to be
Illegal.

When you don't realise
What you could have done,
It breaks down into nothingness,
Expectations vanquished and torn apart
From old dreams, ancient realities
Beyond human nature and unreality.

What are you supposed to be?
One never knows, until the last call,
Ever changing, flexible direction
Over the mind and the will,
Unceasing and relentless to explore,
To dare beyond human experience,
Always limited, always so fragile,
Impotent in the face of so many
Unknown challenges.

Despair and uncertainty take control
Over the many absent-minded,
Unsure and unsafe in their beliefs.
Tremble and shaken beyond explanation,
Get sucked by the ruthless, demanding
And ever present bureaucratic society,
Too concerned in keeping appearances
And figures in contended statistics,
Always eager to prove a point
But useless in human dignity.

9/02/06

Wandering

Nowhere else to be found
Nowhere else to go to
But inside my mind
I see you walking by
Taking and following
The same footsteps
You once walked
Bewilders me with stupefaction
Whirling inside my own self
Lost in between dreams and visions
Reflections upon a quiet inner lake
Torn apart from the obviousness
Of a stare
Caught in between two worlds
Two realities or unrealities
Swept away by a breathtaking
Quiet sound
Coming from the depths
Of the Higher Self
Longing and yearning
For Oneness
For comfort and care
Diving into old and ancient memories,
Misty and imperceptible
In a dim flow of purity
Of integrity and love
For all that once was
And still yearns to be
Free!

Free at last?
Fulfilled and made whole

Again?
Oh, eternity longing to perceive,
Wings of a hopeful wind,
Aspiring to achieve it...

And so it never dies
It keeps on dwelling within
Wandering beneath the surface
Of a quiet sea
Vast and deep
Never ceasing to flow
To wave back and forth
Delivering messages and feelings
To the surfaced self
Awakening it to astounding
Truths and realities
Never again to be
Misled and baffled,
Dissipating the greyness and
The darkness
Of misguided notions
And artificial dogmas,
Bound by ancient and misused
Man-made laws
Who impoverish perception
And deny a coming back,
Experience and communion
Of old times
For old times' sake...

10/02/06

The Quest

There was a profound reverence for pain
For he had known what he had felt
Within his chest
Only revered and searched for
In the most inner sanctum of all things.

He had known, he had wanted to show
The mystery of the ancient legend
A torn-apart secrecy untold
Never unveiled until there came a moment
When a truer heart revealed itself
Never again to be forsaken
By the majesty of Man
Sought for, wished for
In a quest for the ultimate answer
Never before released...

21/06/06

Glimpses of Oneness

The strongest desire of all ages
Has been the quest for eternal bliss
No matter how it was sought or achieved
The bond between Man and the Universe
Always dreamt and aspired
Has produced countless visionaries and dreamers
Seeking to attain infinity through inner attunement
Outwardly transpiring glimpses of Oneness
Fragments of the Wholeness of Cosmos
Travelling through time and space
Shattering dogmas and institutionalized creeds
Freeing the Soul towards the Higher Self
Releasing ideas and visions
To awaken Mankind from lethargy and oblivion
The downward spiral of mere satisfaction
Never permanent, never fully satisfactory.

21/12/06

Simplicity

Simplicity wanders
Through the midst of our minds
Searching for a shelter
Where to dwell upon.

Delivery of the Spirit
Of communion,
Of reunion with the Self,
Longing to attain
A more constant contact
With reality
Embedded without illusion,
Withholding the veils
That dim and blur the Mind
In its everlasting quest for Oneness.

Let go, let the flow of your being unfold
Naturally, without effort
Like the lotus flower blossoms
From the mud of earthly passions
And reaches high in the world.

In its effortless movement
It marvels and surprises the Soul
Every step of the Path
Towards Self realization
Without end...

14/09/07

Kaleidoscopic visions

The power of the spoken word
Flows softly but firmly
Through the space between us both
Permeating the air
Like a swift and steady breeze
And it lingers and awakens certain senses
Within us
Which deepen hidden certainties
Of lost mysteries
Of who we truly are and should be.

The flow of consciousness
Runs free and wild
Seeking a way to express itself
Through motions and notions
Of what is
And what is not
Projecting beams of light and wisdom
Reflecting the need to illuminate
From the inside out
In a kaleidoscopic spectrum of multiplicity
Assuming many aspects of the Self
Dissipating the mist of doubt and blunder
Attaining the expression of clarity and belief
Unveiling the real nature of maturity
In the stream of consciousness...

25/12/07

What must come to pass

I have been wanting to know
What is the meaning of all of this.
Sensing the changes
Sensing the inner challenges
Roaring from the inside out
Making themselves visible, physical,
Upsetting the mind and body.

Are they warnings?
Are they knocks on my door?
Awakening signs, probably…

Wake up!
Open your inner eyes
Open your heart and soul
And let them flow freely.
Get rid of the burdens and tensions
Of the past, of old habits
And be free once again
Truly, completely unbound
Without the limitations
Of mere humans
Without the limited scope of physicality
Unshackle your will and vision
Behold the greatness of Life
In every passing moment
In every single day
And you will achieve the summit
Of Self-realization
Not for your self
But for all mankind
Raising its consciousness

To a higher degree
Achieving its vital potential
Of what must come to pass.

If it is destined
If it is meant to be
Then, why wait?

Come, ye stranger
Come and unite now.
It is time.
It is the moment
Right as it always is.

Then, why bother worrying?
No need for that waste of energy.
Let it flow
Let the flow of Life
Pass through you
And be transfigured.

It is done
It is finished
It is sealed.
Let it be as it is.
Forever.
Free.
Whole.
Yes.
Definitely.

29/12/07

Life as it is

Each one must go about one's business
And that's for sure
When you stop to wonder
About what Life is
In its myriad forms and shapes
Colours and shades
Never knowing nor realizing
How big it really is
In its diversity
The crossing and uncrossing of paths
Each one leading to a different place
Each one with a different purpose
Saying "Hi!" occasionally
Stopping for a moment or two
But never ceasing to flow...

Do we dare stopping?
We mustn't
For there is a golden pot
At the end of the rainbow
And there's one for everyone
Who defies and surpasses
The dark side of the soul
The unfolding of spirals and spirals
Labyrinths within labyrinths
Which appear along the way within
Bringing forth potential and opportunities
Ready for the picking
If you are on the right spot
At the right moment
And if you dare accepting it as yours...

Keep on dreaming, my boy
Keep on letting your mind wonder
About the nature of things
But be damned ready to absorb it fully
Or prepare to die from within...

11/01/08

Change

People change...
But sometimes they don't...
And sometimes they can't...
Although they must...
Or at least they should...

Change is upon us
All the time...
Sometimes we don't see it
Some other times we can't perceive it.

But changing we must
Or ought to
Because if we don't
Life will change us
Not always (or almost never)
In the most agreeable way...
Yes, changing, but in what direction?
For the better, not for the worse
Definitely.

Agreed. But what is the right way?
To the right, to the left, up or down?
Straight forward, unquestionably.

Life does not rest, it keeps on moving.
So, moving we must be
No matter where to
As long as we keep up with the flow...

28/06/08

Confrontation

The course of events
Is set.
No matter what was done
Or will be
The game has begun.

And many consequences have arisen
The action was put forth
The players are ready to begin
The final confrontation.

Strategies are set into action
The dice have been released
Fame and tale
Will be recalled and recorded
For future generations.

The moves are made
Each one follows one's rule
Not always the same
Styles mix and confront each other
In a battle for supremacy.

Who shall overcome all the others?
The most passionate one
The most skilful one
The most strong-minded one?
Or the most simple and purest at heart?

The final verdict is uncertain
The last moment unattained.
Must we fight a good fight?

Or must we abstain
From confrontation?

28/06/08

Being

How can we be ourselves
Without being?
Is it worth changing
For the sake of others?

In a multiple reality of Beings
Being who we are
Means confronting other perceptions
Of the world?

Who must we please
Our own identity
Or the way others see us?
And how do they perceive who we are?
Through physical eyes
But also through the inner eye
Of the soul.

And what perception of us
Reflects towards the outside?
Is it the real thing
The real us?
Or merely a glimpse
Of what we truly are?

What about our own Self?
Do we really know it?
Have we ever come into contact
With it?

Notions of a dimmed twilight area
Perceptions of a hidden abstract reality

Always looking for our identity
Never ceasing to exist
In a timeless quest for eternity...

28/06/08

Acting

Life is a dream
Mostly dreamt with eyes shut.
But sometimes
Glimpses and visions appear
Disturbing and confusing
What was meant to be reality.

What must we trust?
The evident facts
Brought about by our physical senses
Or the subtle feelings, fragrances, sounds and colours
That sometimes arise?

When we stop living for a few moments
In the normal flow of events
And we ponder upon what is inside
We see a scene being set forth
Pre-disposed in advance
With a known cast and set
With a pre-conceived plot
We can detach ourselves from it
And watch it from the outside.

That is when realization comes
And doubts become certainties
And we truly come to understand
What the meaning really is...

That we are all actors on a stage
Performing the roles of a lifetime
Pretending to be someone
Acting as if we were unaware

Of the greatest picture of all –
Reality!

28/06/08

Sharing

Wanting to share
Dreams, hopes and expectations
About Life in its multiplicity
How sweet and gentle it is
To slowly savour the beauty of it all
To silence the outward senses
And then plunge inwardly
Towards the very core of Being
Expecting to attain the highest perceptions
Ever experienced and shared
The magnitude of yonder heights
The dazzlement achieved
Surmounts and surpasses
Anything tangible and physical
Entering the realm of fairies
And mystical beings of Light
The glitter and sparkling atmosphere
Floods my entire Self
And I long to maintain
This weightlessness dimension
Of it all...

17/07/08

Multitude

There are moments
When I feel an urge
To shout out loud
My love for the world!

I observe it carefully
I try to absorb
Each and every aspect of it
And I long to live many lives
At the same time
Wishing to experience all
There is to be experienced
And my mind wanders erratically
Through gusts of wind and light
Aspiring to breathe in every atom and molecule
Wanting to expand the consciousness
Of being alive completely!

I wish I could spread my thoughts
As beacons of light
Tiny pieces of me
Fragments of my own self
Yearning to breathe free
Towards the endless out there
Without limits or restrictions
Just dreaming, hoping and aiming
To grasp the wholeness of reality.

Is it possible?
How is it feasible?
Is it a path worth walking?
The soul is an ever-wishing entity

Craving to attain unspoken truths
Needing it as much as fresh air
Aspiring for it desperately
Just to live...

19/07/08

Awakening

Questioning Life as it is
Brings us to a point
Where answers are not always clear
Where questions are never easy to ask
And when it comes to the bottom line
There is much to be said
To be sought
To be pondered...

Should we question Life?
Or should we just live it
Fair and square?

But we are more than dummies
And so we owe much
To our inner selves
To that voice that sometimes
Makes itself heard
Feebly, timidly, many times dormant...

And when it makes itself heard
Great moments arise
Like a magnificent dawn
When clarity overshadows all obscurity
And forgotten dreams come forth to life
Awakened by beams of consciousness
In its pure yet simple essence
Shedding conscious determination
To a once sleepy mind
Transfiguring and recreating
The course of events
Lit by awareness and clarity
And setting things back on track...

Who are we, really?
Where are we headed to?
Ah, who wants to know?
I do...
Ok... that's the way things are...
You've got a question...
I give you an answer
And things keep on flowing...
Always...

12/11/08

Surrendered

Joyful bliss
Pounds in one's heart
When Life is seen as a whole
And it is unveiled
Before our bare eyes
What playful and colourful vision
There is to be seen
Savoured and tasted
With full senses
Wide open with arms
And heart and body
Absorbing it fully
Through our skin
Being run through by reality
In such a gentle yet steady way
Like a soft summer breeze
Caressing our hair and face
With tender hands
Filling our beings into the core
Overcoming our entire perception
Leaving no one untouched.

What must we do, then?
Nothing, besides being receptive
In a childlike manner
Taking inside every moment
Retaining each passing second
With bewilderment
In complete awe
Marvelled by such splendour
Grandiose symphony
Played with simplicity

With utter attention
For every detail must count
In our quest for belonging
And for being
Wholefully One with Life...

14/12/08

Together as one

When we, together as brethren
Shall envision the higher purpose
Of our nation
Then we shall overcome
Our inner limitations
Our misconceptions
Our fears and uncertainties
And so we will head
Towards our destiny
Shielded by the armour
Of honour and of fate
Higher than anything before seen
In our midst
In our hearts and souls.

It will be therefore
Ready to pick
Taken and assumed
As rightfully ours
Forever without any shadow of doubt
And of shame of any ancient wrong doing
For it is certain that one day
We shall overcome
What must be surpassed
Left behind without remorse
Unmistakably sure
Of the right path
That only free men and women
Dare walk as theirs
From this moment on…

Unquestionably?
Yes, undoubtedly ours
By our own legacy and right!

14/12/08

Golden opportunity

Time travelling
Can become a deception
When one visits old memories
And finds them lurking behind
Rags and fragments of old ages
Torn apart by the passing of time
On and on insisting upon reviving
Dreams and wishes
Wrinkled by the never ceasing
Flow of time
That ruthless carrier of misfortune
And decay
Affecting us all
Relentlessly...

Yet it brings wisdom
And clarity of mind
Dignity and providence
Dissipating the notion of oblivion
A reward-like promise
Of entering a dawning golden age
Preparing to accept a quantum leap
Bound to happen very soon
Alerting the mind and body
To plunge into a silvery network of conscience
Empowering the soul
Towards higher octaves of consciousness
Revealing truths and mysteries alike
For the gathering of collective unity
Mankind awakened
From forgetfulness and abandonment
Of all age realities and certainties

Returned to the path of enlightenment
Through self-knowledge
Aspiring for dwelling and living
In harmonious bliss...

15/12/08

Frantic living

Taking care of only one thing
At the same time
As we try to do so many things
Is our daily challenge
Our trial for being considered
Effective and professional.

But what do we lose
In the mean time?
So much...
Only if we could perceive it...

But do we have a choice?
No, we don't
Because we can't stop
Must rush
All day long
Despite the confusion and stress
We must prove
We are chaos-proof
And nothing will affect us!

But are we really?
I'm afraid that's not the case...

And then a pounding heart
Beats in unison with the mind
Blood runs wild through arteries and veins
Stomach and gut get squeezed
Moving hands and feet
Run wild and frenzy
And in the mean time

A frantic being struggles
To stay alive
To get things going
Seeking desperately
For a safe haven
To calm down
To relax
To rest
To stop…
Until when?

16/12/08 – 23/12/08

Unlimited quest

What have we got to do with pleasure?
What is it, anyway?
It is different for everyone
That's for sure!

But there must be a common link
A certain pattern
That runs through us all
Which determines how far
Each one of us is determined to go
Just to get it.

People feel pleasure
In so many different ways
With so many different stimuli
That it seems difficult
To agree universally upon it.

The pleasure for taste
The pleasure for touch
Definitely two of the strongest ones
But there is also bewilderment
In seeing
And unlimited amazement
In listening
As well as delightfulness
In smelling
The exquisite, delicate and soft fragrances
Admiring the wonderful and the simple sounds
And gazing the breathtaking images
That we are surrounded by.

And are we ever pleased
Fully satisfied?
Never, because we are always eager
For more and more...

Yet it is so simple
To be completely reassured
If we dare content with few
There will always be plenty
If our measure is low
Then we will always be full
Specially if we plunge inwards
Exploring sights and sounds within
Or just silence and stillness
The emptiness of the void
Allowing nothingness
To be fulfilled
To the utmost experience
Of all
Being made whole
In a fragment of time and space
Inexplicably
Unreliably
Uncertainly
Undone yet so much complete...

Should there be a quest for something?
Yes, for the unquest...

16/12/08

The second coming

He, who comes at a time
Not yet known
Except by the heart and soul
Brings hope and faith
In the Order of the Universe
In the coming together of brethren
In the union and communion
Of the human race
Bringing forth from the heart of each one
Love, understanding, concern for all
And united we shall become
Never again separated nor apart
Because we are truly one Being
One Body upon this Earth
And the Light shining forth from within
Shall prevail in the end
And small egos shall crumble down
And only the manifestation of the Spirit
Shall be heard
Shall be seen
And people will begin to hear and to see
The greatest picture of all
And Light shall descend
Upon this celestial body
Melting away all doubt and fear
Sharing Peace and Love
Conquering all shadows and darkness
By the simple bright shining Light
Altering all perception
Changing all notions
Transforming the old into the new
Free at last from ancient bondage!

Be prepared, ye brethren
He shall soon come...

24/12/08

Dream Catcher

I embark on a vision quest
Detached from all dogmas and limitations
I envision the white cloud high in the sky
The bald eagle soars into the blue
Dominating all below
Perceptions arise from within
Inner boundaries are challenged and overcome
The grizzly bear stretches his might in the forest
The owl catches glimpses of reality
And intuitive feelings and images
Flood me with power, harmony and a belief
In the presence of the Great Spirit
Who permeates us all
With a gentle touch
Like the soft breeze
And a strong presence
Like the thunder and the lightning
Giving life to all sentient beings
And the whole of Nature
Rejoices with the abundant pouring rain
A gift from the sky
Uniting us all
Brothers and sisters
In the Web of Life!

12/01/09

Winter glitter

Memories from the old Spring mountain
Surge from my being
Now, in the stillness of Winter
The cold, freezing, numb landscape
Shines forth in a bright blinding white
No movement occurs
Except from within
In the distance
All is pale
Snowy flakes fall heavily
Making hard and harsh all life
Prey and hunter lay dormant
Waiting for Spring
To allow for any activity
Lurking patiently
Every day
Until the season changes
And Life starts bursting out
Expanding outwards
In a limitless movement
Always forward
Once again brought back to life
And the melting of the white
Snow and ice dissolve into clearness
Flowing streams, creeks and rivers
Dump their Winter load
Into lightness
Soft moving motion
Becomes strong flowing freedom
Expanding its evermore presence
Allowing green pastures to grow
Blooming Nature expands effortlessly into colours

A once still and void realm
Brought back to Life and motion!

15/01/09

Watching, just watching

I cannot be someone else
I cannot live somebody else's life
But sometimes
I feel my mind drifting away
From my being
Wandering aimlessly
Through the world
Attempting to scan
Through other people's eyes
Their posture, their stare
And the way they look
Inside and outside
Appearances deceive the attentive eye
And they come and go
All different but all the same...

Do they question themselves
As I do?
What images and sensations
Go through their hearts?
Do they perceive reality
As a fluid, moving web
Always intertwined
With each other
By invisible threads of light?

No certainties
Some expectations
So many doubts...

15/01/09

Buddha's eyes

Stillness flickering in one's eyes
Casts out all fears and doubts
Caresses the soul with delight and awe
Reaches for the utmost feeling of oneness
And realises that all is in its right place
And acceptance is the key to illumination...

1/02/09

One's way

Self-discipline is the engine for success
Or is it not?
When one cares about things
Diligently
And orderly
Things go smoothly
And evenly
And life keeps rolling on track...

But what if one isn't prone
To do that
Cutting some slack
Giving some latitude
To do things
And being less willing
To be Mr. Perfect
All the time?

Is precision
The only way
For getting things right?

Letting things flow
Not too anxious about the outcome
Or at least about getting things done
For yesterday
Can be a more relaxed and creative way
Of watching the film unfold
Before our very eyes
As a watcher, not a doer
But as a character, still
In the course of events.

What are we aiming at?
What are we aiming for?

Experience things
In every possible way
In every possible way
Not only in the right way
But also in a certain way
One's way...

1/02/09

Hide and seek

Hiding and seeking…
Which one shall prevail?
Who or what are you hiding from?
Who or what are you seeking?
Which of the two shall overcome the other?
Which one is the strongest?
Which one runs deeper in your veins?

Hiding does not lead you far
Because wherever you go
Whatever you do
You will always be found.
Your identity cannot be hidden
Nor mistaken by anybody else's.
It is something you will always
Have to claim as rightfully yours.

You can never hide from your Self
For it is always there, in you
Present in your heart…

So why don't you keep on seeking?
There is always the ultimate Quest
Waiting to be rekindled
To be resumed, exactly where you left it…

And you cannot escape your destiny
Your higher goal in Life
To be a seeker, a finder of the Truth
To unite once more with the Answer
The very same one that has faced you
Over and over again

Lifetime after lifetime
Bringing you back to heights of glory
Of attunement
Of harmony
And of synchronicity with the Cosmos
In a timeless moment
On a formless place
Of nowhere and everywhere
Shattering illusion
And becoming Whole again...

Seek and ye shall find...

12/04/09

Out of Time

Time, ruthless time
Never stopping
Never ceasing to flow
Running away
Towards an unknown destiny
Escaping all attempts
To be bound
To be stopped
To be dominated
By will
To be slowed down
To be savoured
Instead of being
Run over by it...

Taking time
Seriously
Is a way of making more
Out of it
Instead of being deprived
Of it
By choice and by desire
To accept it as it is
And by stopping for a while
Being able to surrender
To a deep down sense
Of detachment
Of letting go
Now and then always
In order to be free
Ultimately free
From its ever present flow

That ruthless ticking
Which deprives me
Of so many things...

Yet, resistance builds up
Creating an unwinding effect
And a counter-clock motion
Begins to take place
And time recedes back
Slowly but patiently
Allowing changes to occur
Within and without
Assuming any form nor shape
It transforms reality
Into something different
Enabling more in less
A conscious intent
Sets into motion
An unconscious effect
Making a deeper and longer voyage
Into nothingness
Creating a void-like feeling
Yet so full and so vibrant...

25/04/09

Within Time

A chasm in time
Isn't always
What we expect it
To be
It may strongly indicate
That we were not capable
Of finding the right moment
The right time
And we plunge into the vast
Nothingness
And nothing stays the same...

Misconceptions
Preconceptions
Premeditation never occurs
Or at least it shouldn't
But then we are all alone
And that's merely a fact of Life
That when we cry
Maybe there is no one
Out there
To hear our pledge
Towards a higher purpose
In a limitless world of form
Of thought, of mind
And a pure sense of weightlessness
Floods my being
Completely
And so Time
Makes haste
Without reflecting upon
The vast sorrow

Which anticipates
What is to come
Soon, so soon...

21/05/09

One and the same

Wise men say
That sacred words
Must not be forgotten
Nor forsaken
Nor rebuked by any one
Because it is in moments
Of peril
Of distrust
And of misconduct
That righteousness
Must be forged
In the furnace of the mind
The will and the heart
Shall always prevail
Few among many
Will devise and foresee
The upcoming of days
New revelations torn apart
By savants, by masters
Of the Light
And they shall unveil
The unseen, the untouched
Because it has been hidden
Deep down inside
Where no one could have suspected
And thus within
In the bosom of flesh and blood
Lies the most revered and sacred
The *Spiritus Sanctus*
Gathered and made whole
In Man and Woman alike
The rightful heirs of the legacy

Of the sky and of the heavens
United once more
To bring forth the answer
The key to a long sought
Quest for holiness or wholeness
One and the same
Finally put.

Bewilderment?
Always renewed...

12/06/09

Ultimate freedom

The one who is free
But does not use his freedom
To be absolutely free
Ultimately free
Inside and outside
Has not yet found
The true essence of that freedom.

He must then be possessed
By an unbreakable will and spirit
To go beyond the obvious
To stare and gaze the true colours
Of his inner being
Dwindling and waving away
Into the core of reality
And so, by shutting the outer senses
The inner senses bloom
Allowing perceptions to dawn
Enabling the mind
To observe
To absorb
To be cuddled
And to savour
The full spectrum of delight
Whirling softly within
Seizing the pinnacle of existence
In such a simple and blissful way
Yet unknown before
Wave upon wave
Floods the astounded being with amazement
Suddenly coming to terms with his freedom

And finally realizes and experiences
The true meaning of Liberty...

2/07/09

The Nonconformist

Nonconformism is a virtue
Or is it a plague?
As always, it depends
On the point of view.

Speaking your peace
Mostly in a revolutionary way
Tends to attract
A great deal of opposition
From the mainstream
Unwilling to lose rights
And to allow contention
Over the *status quo*
Of institutionalized creed and deed...

Therefore, trying to change
The state of current affairs
Awakens the beast
And any attempt to challenge them
Faces dire consequences
Preventing people from realizing
And conceiving their full potential.

However, some manage to slip
Under their ruler's reach
And expand their true nature
Nurturing and nourishing
Their essence and valour
Daring to aspire to new heights
Glory and grandeur awaiting to be reached
Setting new foundations for a new world order

Enabling a new dawn to emerge
And breaking down the shackles of deceit and ignorance...

5/08/09

Confirmation

Walking by the lake shores
I sense marks of cognition
In every footstep taken
And as I realize what is happening
I enter a new realm of perception
New dimensions emerge
In front of my bare eyes
And I become aware of new impressions
That fill my being with a pallet of colours
And I am struck and transfigured
By endless waves of sound and light
In a surprising symphony
Which bathes and caresses my entire being...

The notion of time is lost completely
When I attempt to grasp and to hold on to
This out of the body experience
And so I begin to understand
From within and without
Any shadow of doubt
I am free to perceive
Other dimensions out there
Only if I am willing
To let my self flow freely
And accept truly, without questioning
What I am offered every step of the way
Any time, anywhere
Until I finally realize
That I am not merely this body
But I am many beings in one
Only for now, for this time travelling
And the answer to existing uncertainties

Lies just ahead, along the path
And existence is simply
A quest for self-discovery...

2/08/09

Equine bond

Majestic being
Galloping wild and free
Along the vast long prairie
Its mane hovering in the wind
Leaving behind traces of its existence
I am touched by its presence
And its aura of animal magnetism
Contrasts with its poise and splendour
Making my dreams and aspirations
Desiring to be in your midst
Aspiring to voyage on a journey
Of communion together
Longing for a life-long commitment
Of companionship, of trust
Aiming to attain your elegance
Your royal fascinating charm
Man and stallion
United forever
On spacious fields of eternity...

2/08/09

Stunning doubt

Not letting you down...
Is down necessarily bad?
Is high necessarily good?
What about in between?
A balance?
What kind of balance?
The one sought for
Aspired for, dreamt of
The one that is so perfect
That nothing else can be added to it...

How do we let someone down?
Not fulfilling expectations?
Why are we always having second thoughts?
Should we expect anything
From anyone?
So it seems...
We are dependent beings
Battered, scared, lonely...
You name it!
And that's how the game is...

Excuse me? What game?
Are you insane?
This isn't a game
This is me, myself
We're talking about!
I count, so don't you talk to me like that!

I'm sorry
Maybe I'm not
In the right place
At the right time.

Let me rephrase it:
Are you talking *about* me?
Then, oblige me
With some decency
And dignity
Because I deserve it.

Yes, you do, more than anyone else.

So, is it possible to get
Some real attention from you?
The way you've changed...
Don't you see we are going
In different directions?

I *do* care about you
But sometimes
I kind of forget your needs
And I let my upside world
To be turned upside down
In between a stare and a glass of water
Dwelling thoughts arise to the surface
And then I dive into them
Into me and my fluid world
Where nothing ever has a shape
Things are never
What they are supposed to be...
And I get lost in between
Two worlds apart
And my reality
Becomes the unreality
Of flashes, glimpses, intuitive insights
That fulfil me
When I'm there
Whenever I need an escape

I'm there
So I forget
Or I don't remember
Basic, solid things anymore...
It's not that I don't care
It's more that
I can't help it...

But, eventually
I come back
At least once a day
Trying to grab and catch
Bits and pieces left on the floor
And I do my best
To make some sense out of them
My best... not the *perfect* way
But sincere
And I try to make things
Whole again...

31/08/09

The notion of poetry

What is poetry?
Poetry cannot be prescribed
Only described
Felt intensely
Through the filter of the heart
And of the soul
In magnified images
Not in black and white
But in bright, stunning, shining colours!

And how does one
Apprehend reality?
Simply by shutting down the mind
And turning on all the senses
Breathing in deeply
And letting the emotions
Fly wild and free
Unquestioning what appears
No matter how weird
Or how futile it all seems
That is the beauty
Of it all
How genuine one can be
When emotions get expressed
Into words
And how sad it is
When people are not aware at all
Of it all...

Then one must realize
How it all is
And materialize

Precarious notions
Into the world of form
Through impressions
As vivid as possible
But never as solid as rocks
Because some space
Must be left in between
To be filled by people's essence
Allowing them to absorb poetry
As much as they can
But at their own pace
Slowly and patiently
Eroding misconceptions
Stone-hard values
Become lighter and softer
And rigidity of mind and heart
Is appeased and enlightened
Transfiguring people from within
Dissipating little by little
The veils of illusion
From true seekers of beauty and light...

7/09/09

Transmutation

Say it out loud
Bluntly, without masks
Nor hesitations
Whenever you wish for
The truth to be uttered
Not murmured softly
And you shall feel
At peace
With your self
Because you might have felt
That you were devastated
By severe consequences
For your upheaval.

But you must face
Your dark corners
Your less beautiful facets
If you want to redeem yourself
From some obscure part of you
And therefore you must shed light
And lightness into everything you do
Everything you say and think
And laughter shall be upon you
And joy shall flood you completely
Your entire being shedding the old aside
Casting away all darkness and obscurity
Allowing you to transform and transcend
The lead of lower emotions and feelings
Transmuting it into the gold of higher consciousness
In the alchemy of the Self
Where shadows fade away
And illumination emerge

Leaving behind old patterns and dogmas
Breaking down resistance
And exerting your resilience
Once more, again and again...

09/03/09 – 17/09/09

All different, all equal

One cannot assume
That one is superior
Or inferior to anyone
In any way, shape or form
No matter what
Colour or sex
Race or faith
Weight or height
Sexual orientation or creed
Rich or poor
Young or old
Because we are one and the same
We share the same heritage
Exterior differences mean nothing
The human race's DNA
Is imprinted upon each
And everyone of us
And so we are all connected
Despite the immense diversity of ethnicity
We commune from the same principles
From the same deep down values
Being bonded by indestructible ties
All together
In a tremendously challenging human adventure
So many times on the brink of calamity
Brought about by mad ideologies
Creating so much suffering
To so many millions of innocent beings
Even today, at the dawn of a new era
There is still so much pointless violence
So much injustice in a so-called modern world
Such few opportunities and little comfort for so many

That it is our unalienable duty
As citizens of the world
To care for the famished
For the sick and the underprivileged
Because we owe it to our common origin
We owe it to our own true selves
To be the forerunners of peace and justice
To become bringers of hope and freedom
For tomorrow's generations...

Let there be an awakening of consciousness
In all those who can
Because there are too many who cannot
And one day we shall be accountable
For turning our faces aside...

18/09/09

Heartbroken

Looking frail and pale
Scared and lonely
Lost without a compass
You refuse to live life
As the free person
You were forced to become
And you still feel stuck
To a love long gone
Despised and replaced
By another woman
But always trying and tempting
Your weakness
And making you suffer
Keeping you waiting
Suspended in mid-air
Longing for moments
Long gone
Aspiring to gain self-control
But always failing
Falling into temptation
Failing to regain your life back
Letting time still go by
Leaving a bleeding heart
Pointlessly unhealed...

And thus, suffering still
Carries on and on
And each passing day
Does not bring anything
Nor anyone new
Because you are shut
From the inside

Wanting but unwilling
To let go
Incapable of realizing
That chapters come to an end
And new ones begin
Only if we are willing
To keep on turning the pages
And allowing Life to take control
Instead of letting someone
The character from an earlier play
Continuing to haunt the present
With past memories
Instead of shutting him out
And wilfully cutting all ties
From someone who is
Nothing but a ghost
A mere spectre
Demanding a strong measure
A decisive attitude
Casting him aside for good
And starting to live free
Free from emotional bondage
Ready to accept the new reality
And allowing unpredictability
Into your life and being
Accepting joyfully what might come...

Awaken and be free
Free at last...

3/10/09

The falling of the veils

Wherever we look at
Everything and everyone
Has an inner beauty
Even if on the outside
Appearances aren't that beautiful
But what truly matters
Is not "what you see is what you get"
On the contrary
"What you see, you ain't seen nothing!"
Until you look further away
Beyond obvious expectations
Things that are hidden inside
Until you voluntarily dim your outer sight
And turn on the inner eye
Focusing on the essence
What is not showing but it's there…

If you pause for a second
Inner sights and impressions begin to appear
And letting them flow
Flooding our intuitive being
In such a strong way
The mind is blown away
By beacons of light
Nothing logical nor reasonable
Appears softly and slowly
And then we realize
Truth as it really is
And so we come to terms
With the ever-present impression
Of compassionate being
A non-biased approach

Towards Life in general
And people in particular
As we come to the utter realization
That we are surrounded by beauty
In all things, all phenomena, all people
And prejudice and distrust
Crumble away
And a new age of love and trust
In our fellow human being arises
And barriers fade away
Ancient hatred melts into nothingness
And people begin looking straight
At each other's eyes
And thus Life is mended
Healed to its former ancient origin
As all become united
Together as brethren...

31/10/09

The quest for art

The art of poetry
Is like
The poetry of art
For the same reason
One cannot judge a book
By its cover
One cannot judge art
By mere contemplation
Of the portrait of the artist
Always ahead of his time
Seeing over the present
In search for a future to be
Attempting to create
A new reality
Trying hard to go beyond conventions
Always aiming to break down rules
Always pushing forward to innovate
And a fine piece of art
Begins to be born
Creation takes place in every breath taken
Nothing stays the same
As the artist impresses her soul
Into forms and colours
Sounds and images
Shaping of raw materials does occur
And a new concept of reality eventually appears
Creating a new dimension for people to reach
Transforming both the world and the viewer
Because reality is made by what is observed
Making new things happen
Enriching people's perception
Expanding limitless possibilities

The artist is never pleased
For the world must be redesigned
And much is still undone
Before one's purpose is accomplished...

The poetry of art
Is always being moulded and expanding
For the quest for the ultimate master-piece
Is never completed...

2/11/09

Unlimited art

The quest for art
Is a quest for self-discovery
Of one's inner boundaries
Trying to go beyond the standards
Through a different set of words
A bold stroke with a brush and colour
A surprising musical arrangement
A harsh shape carved on a stone
Or a different angle caught by a lens
They all tell a different story
A story of survival, of resilience
Of tenacity and vanguardism
Shattering former established dogmas
Aspiring to make a difference
As utopian or unreal as it may be
It creates a new paradigm
Much ahead of its time
So many times misunderstood and confronted
By institutionalized creed
But never weakened
Because free spirits never die
They never surrender
Nor abdicate from their mission
Determined to live and think
By their unpatterns
Unwilling to become
Tagged by any convention
Destined to exert their freedom
Through artistic expression
Awakening people from lethargy
Shaping reality

Into a new era
Yet to appear…

4/11/09

Void

The silence between poems
Speaks for itself...
It has a dimension of its own
And it says more than mere words...
It is the result of deep feelings
Reflections cast down on one's being...

Why should there be an active voice?
Why should there always be
Things to say?
Silence doesn't mean emptiness
It only means patience
Awareness being apparently dormant
Waiting, wanting to surge back again
It means internal conflicts
Being waged on inner battlefields
Awaiting opportunities of speech
To bounce back and forth
To make an impact
On paper and on minds
And, at the end
When it draws near
It doesn't mind the final outcome
As long as it makes a stand
In time and space
Right here, right now
To bring something new
Or at least renewed
For there is always
A new beginning
As it keeps coming back
Between silences and stillness

The emptiness of the void
Is never empty
It is always patiently waiting
To burst out, once again...

Do never assume
That silence is nothingness
It is the hidden growth of a seed
Becoming mature to finally appear
In the daylight of daily events
Of ordinary things always happening
It is growing, becoming bigger and bigger
Stronger and stronger
Until ready to flourish and to be seen...

12/12/09

Merging and adapting

One must mingle, adapt and adjust
Himself to society
In order to keep here
A certain kind of mental sanity
Learning to cope
With established rules and habits
Making himself as "normal" as possible
Being like the bamboo
Which graciously bends and bows
Curved by strong winds
Instead of being like the oak tree
Which tenaciously and stubbornly resists
But then breaks or is ripped out
And tumbles down
Mighty as it was
Loses against a strong opposing tempest...

So one must follow wisdom
Together with flexibility
To be able to absorb and resist
To worldly shocks and storms
Being wise as the water
Which flows and acquires the shape needed
To surpass and surmount perils
Challenges and obstacles
Always aiming to succeed
Leaving behind sheer examples
Of its passing and presence
But also being disastrous
When in anger and in number
Showing that even adaptability

When flooding takes place
Can be as powerful as any hurricane...

26/12/09

Quantum flux

We live in suspended mid-air
Touching lightly on fields of pure energy
Interchanging and interconnecting
On a network of Light
Being all connected
By myriad threads of Love
The reason without human logic
Which binds us all together
Being able to choose
From infinite possibilities
So many times against the odds
A full spectrum of probabilities
Always at our reach
We make options and set standards
Where no patterns are real
Unpredictability is upon us all the time
But time does not exist
So what is left for us?
A dimmed, blurred perception
Watched through finite human eyes
Making perception short and limited
Until the ultimate reality is pierced
New concepts arise
And new sensations appear
And so a new attitude must be assumed
New states of mind burst reality as once known
Creating new concepts, new realities
New beginnings are set from scratch
Into a new multidimensional world
A Universe of endless probabilities
Enabling us to experience countless opportunities
In a living laboratory of quantum experiments
Where intention and free will
Determine the final outcome

Never determined, never fixed
Always open to innumerable expansions of Life
Where no one is apart
One living breathing organism
Oneness and wholeness together
Making all things possible
All things perfect
Even amid imperfectability
All is well, in its true rightful place
In such a tiny fraction of time
Within aeons of cosmic light-years
We are nothing but infants
On a long, long journey
Always aspiring to return Home
OM...
The primordial sound of the Universe
Guiding us back to our source
Our essence and true nature
Among pulsars, nebulae and infinite stars
We come here to claim
What is rightfully ours
Our Solar Logos heritage
We are Children of the Sun
Intergalactic voyagers
On an awesome adventure
From so many different origins
Stellar spirits poured into star dust bodies
We all commune from the same principles
Though scattered but converging to unity
The final outcome soon to be achieved
The gathering of intent and souls
Aiming for the final reunification
One great union
One perfect match
Bound to happen soon, so soon...

31/12/09

Bodhisattva

She, who hears the cries of the world
Is vigilant and takes notice
Of every soul in despair
And comes forth into the Earth
From the other side of the veil
To bring peace and comfort
Enabling and supporting people to endure
To hold on to their hidden strengths
Allowing for dire challenges and conflicts
To be boldly uphold
Caressing and caring for her beloved ones
Humankind as a whole
Only focused on the heart of compassion
Not the skin nor the creed
Collecting and gathering the tears from suffering
And pouring down to the Earth the water of Life
Blessing all with physical and spiritual healing
Vowing to continuously stay behind
To help all undergo travail and worldly burdens
And assist humankind to attain enlightenment...

11/04/10 – 18/4/10

Gathering...

We are a species of gatherers
We gather food, objects and wealth
We collect achievements, deeds and triumph
We accumulate books, diplomas and information
But we are scarce in gathering knowledge, wisdom and
love
We tend to focus too much on the outside
Leaving the inside uncared for...

What is the use of having so much
And possessing so little?
What are we afraid of?
Are we anguished about our own mortality?
Why is our species
So much focused on the individual
And so much alienated on the collective?

It is simply a matter of fact
A warring dominating character
The need to dominate, to possess
The urge to be victor, over and over again
To conquer, to occupy, to own
Leaves no space left
For modesty, humility and caring
For our fellow human being
Especially the down-trodden
The outcasts, the frail and the meek
And so mankind carries on and on
A few exceptions left
Make me still believe
That there is hope
For the future of humankind

'Cause the few that still prevail
Gather not but love
And send it out into the world
Attending the needs of others
Offering smiles and gestures of good will
Being like and mingling with the children
Innocence, passion and a determination
Bound to break barriers, cast down borders and dogmas
Prevailing thoughts of love, happiness and bliss
Melting down fear, hatred and violence
Transforming the Earth from now on
Creating a web of trust, confidence and light
A new age arises, sweeping away old patterns and habits
A new dawn is shared and valued
By the awakened ones, trusting and accepting
A brighter, lighter destiny for man and woman alike
In a network for a new outstanding beginning
Sweeping away all that once was
Setting new limitless standards
And preparing for a giant quantum leap
Stellar bodies emerge from earthen ones
Renewed concepts flood and ignite spirits
Creative imagery redefines reality
Wealth-oriented minds are redesigned
Grandeur and poise shift towards the inside
And a brotherhood of pure souls
Become the only measurable trait
Among people of good will
The only one standing high towards the sky
Their common ground and heritage
Finally back from the stars
Galactic emissaries realizing the Truth
And the world becomes as one...

1/03/10-18/4/10

Cosmic birth

Restrictions, unlimited
Powerful torrent of light
Flooding my being with subtlety
And permeating every pore
Crossing over to the marrow of existence
Never stopping to flow
Never ceasing to exist
Anchored in tiny particles
Undulating photons, shot at the speed of light
Spread throughout the known Universe
Travelling through galaxies, quasars, nebulae
In a wonderful cosmic dance
Flooding and filling each atom of matter
Infusing Life with magnetic vitality
Creating all there is
And establishing the blueprint
For planetary bodies to evolve
And for beings to come into existence
In an astounding cosmic symphony
The music of the spheres
A soundless echo travels
Throughout entire galaxies
And beings are tuned in instantaneously
An energy field so sweet and tender
Yet so powerful and ever present
That begets such an impetus on the Whole
And Life simply happens...

19/5/2010

Ode to a poem never written

It was late, he was tired
No, as a matter of fact
He was exhausted
The day had been long
And full of surprises
And he was anxious to go to bed.

All of a sudden
A line bumped
Into the back of his head
At first, he was thrilled
Even excited
A stream of inspiration
Might come his way!

But then he said, "Nah, that's nothing"
And then, what was supposed to come alive
Was never born, because it was too late
And so it faded away, taken by sleep
Tiredness and disillusion
And so no one would ever
Be carried away
By the depth of its content
The magnitude of its feelings
The grandiose intensity of delight
And so no one would ever
Have their breath taken away
By flamboyant images
Precious pearls would never beseech
The reader's attention and imagination...

And thus lonely it stood
A formless entity
Frail and meek
Not knowing where to go
Where to abide
Indecisive and lost
In a twilight of uncertainty
A mere spectre on the threshold
Of unreality and dreams
Never to be fulfilled...

11/6/2010

Forgetfulness

Automation
Inevitable alienation...

Not thinking, only doing
Performing endlessly, pointlessly
Towards a never existing out there
Without any purpose
But to survive
Not to drown, always struggling
To keep breathing
Above the surface of the water
In a rapids descent
Immersed in strong currents
Bouncing, pounding and smashing you
Ruthlessly, without pauses nor rest
Except in wider streams
Where agitation settles
And tiredness leaves you
With no option but to sleep
A long aspired torpor
That does not last long
And so many other times repeated
Over and over again
Keep coming back
The same pumping adrenaline
The same fighting spirit
And a similar sense of emptiness
Of not living the present moment
Of feeling it intensely
Of grabbing each and every aspect
Of seizing the day completely...

Carpe diem...
Discover and unlock ways
To be bold, daring to express
Your Self entirely
Accessing levels of greater awareness
Of embracing unity and love
For your own sake
For your own soul
That infinite eternal entity
Who is your true you
Who is always patiently waiting
For your lawful reunion
That everlasting match
Without blemish
Without hesitation
Always waiting
Confidently waiting
Knowing in advance
The final outcome
Where no time or space matters
For victory will be certain
Oh yes, so certain...

2/07/10

Rebirth

He was scared.
He was lonely.
He was overwhelmed
By the pain he felt
In his abdomen.

He felt fear
He felt an immense solitude
Even though he was among so many
Like him...

The whiteness around him
Blinded his eyes
Making him suffer
With the coldness
Of oblivion...

His stare, empty and void
Struggled to come back to life
As the days went by
Perhaps trying to mimic
The gentle smiles
And kindness
Around him...

And when he was beginning
To feel a little better
A bit stronger
A new session made him
Vomit his guts
Lose his strengths
Killed his appetite

And plunged his young being
Into sheer despair...

And thus, days and weeks
Passed on and on
As he was being battered
All over...

But slowly, so slowly
His weak hairless figure
Began catching his breath
Regaining strengths
Leaving his paleness behind
Growing new furry hair
And leaving his bed
Starting to play
To smile, to sing
An ode to Life
Brought back from scratch
New opportunities arising
Switching from the frozen livid
Emptiness of white
To the fullness expansion of colours
A vivid explosion of Life!

5/10/2010

The journey within

Those who suffer the agonies of pain
Feel lost and helpless
And search for assistance and comfort
To appease their tribulations
Both physical and emotional
Not realizing that they must
Reflect upon the nature of pain
For it is not merely the outside
But mostly the inside that matters
Where the hidden cause lies
So often a mystery for all
Except for the trained eye
Envisioning the multiple facets
As pieces in a broader puzzle
Fitting perfectly together
Inward reflections
Cast on the outside
Dysfunctions, blockages and unbalances
In the pathways of life and light
Disharmonies on the subtle vital energies
The opposing yet complementary *Yin* and *Yang*
Determine and set the pace
Of cosmic rhythms within
A millennial wisdom still young and bold
Promotes vitality, health and longevity
Through a natural and holistic approach
Stimulating the unconscious healer within
Always ready, always aiming to attain balance
Still aligned with the poet's wisdom
Mens sana in corpore sano
A must for the body and spirit alike
'Cause the secret for wholeness

Is perfect synchronicity
Between body, mind and spirit
And realizing that Life
Is a continuum
That cannot be disrupted
On any level, in any way...

The Mind rules over matter
Determining the blueprint of the body
And how each cell works
With quantum energy waves
Making it all happen
So simple yet in such an intricate way
Consciousness is the ruler of it all
Establishing the pattern
For the flow of energy
Throughout the entire system
Allowing the body to be nurtured
Myriad cells perform a million actions
Evolving silently within us
A great symphony, an ode to joy
And to Life itself...

1/11/2010

Afterword

Why I write (or why writing happens through me)

Writing does not happen because of a conscious intention; writing happens because there is a need to express feelings, thoughts or sensations. Usually, it happens because of a certain event which creates the need to reflect upon it. Events, in themselves, are not important, but are pieces of a big puzzle that make our own existence complete. So, each event becomes an important element, brought upon a moment in time, which calls for my attention and unleashes the potential for inner reflection, which is then exteriorized by the "inner sense", the voice of the unconscious.

In this way, the object is analysed from one or more angles, and it becomes a very special phenomenon, which generally (always, as a matter of fact!) has two opposing polarities, or tendencies. So, quite often, the reflection establishes a contrast / comparison between those polarities, trying to make some sense out of it. Then, what "comes out" is a sort of a painting, built with words which try to describe not merely the "outside", the visual aspects, but specially and mostly, the "inside", the hidden reality as I see it.

The result is a "wandering path" in search for the "essence" of the object being observed or reflected upon. Sometimes, it is like a story, in which what is important are not the characters or the plot, in themselves, but what lies underneath of them. The words, then, try to convey the impressions that they produce, on an unconscious level, and what is written is many times less important than what is left unsaid, created by the blank inner spaces, which in turn will facilitate and expand the future reader's own free interpretation and thoughts.

Unconscious notions and schematics can influence and permeate the unconscious mind of the reader and produce images, feelings, sensations and thoughts. All of these, hopefully, will make some sense and may enable the reader to have his/her own thoughts and reflections on that object, allowing and calling his/her attention towards an element, part of the big puzzle of Life and existence.

Inspiration comes in many ways: through watching people in the tube ("Madness", "The blind man", and "Puzzlement"), after watching a film ("Yonder love", "Suicide" and "The Nonconformist"), watching people in a supermarket ("Watching, just watching"), during meditation retreats ("Simplicity" and "Buddha's eyes") and after having watched an art exhibition ("The quest for art" and "Unlimited art"). The rest of them come "out of the blue", literally! The title of a poem may come to my mind one or two weeks before the poem itself, not having the slightest clue of what it will be about ("Jasmine drops"), sometimes I feel an urge to write about a certain topic ("Freedom", "Depression", "Smoking life away", "Heartbroken", "Void", "Ode to a poem never written", "Rebirth" and "The journey within") but having to wait for the right moment, for the right "inspirational mood", after ideas have gathered in my mind until ready to be written. However, the most recurring writing method consists of, in the middle of anything, the first line comes to my conscious mind, I sit down to write it straight away, and then the second comes, and the next and all the rest keep on coming without ceasing, and without any interference, until the poem is complete. At the end of all the writing, I come up with the title, usually after having read the poem once and making myself conscious of what it really is about.

The writing process helps me to exorcise my doubts, my expectations, my "permanent wondering attitude", and it becomes vital for my mental sanity to express whatever flows in my mind through words. Writing unleashes a power that wouldn't come into the world of form if it wasn't for this process of materializing and organizing the flow of thought. Writing is always a magical journey, a quest for something that is almost never clear at the beginning of a poem. And I am never aware how far my writing will take me, both in terms of length as well as in the development of the topic. Until there is "steam", until there is still a path to walk, until there are doubts or questions to be asked, writing will keep on going, taking me further and further away. This will continue until there is a warning sign, that the end is near. Questions raised in the beginning lead many times to questions asked at the end. That is how, without a conscious intent, I explore a topic, trying to make some sense out of it and, at the very end, I leave a question "floating in the air", to be taken by the reader, to let him/her the responsibility for finding the solution for it or making him/her wonder about the final outcome. Some other times, writing happens as a way of cherishing Life, as a way of expressing my uttermost awe at the magnitude and beauty of both the world of form and the archetypes behind it. I expect that, during that process, I might achieve something agreeable to be read later on, hopefully leaving some impressions on the mind and heart of the readers to be.

This book of poems is organized in chronological order and the date when each poem was written is mentioned. Well, the date isn't that important but it is interesting (at least for me) to see how often poems were written, in a very "frugal" way, during the first years, and how they have been increasing in number and frequency in recent years, especially in 2008 and 2009. Some poems have two dates, the first date is when it was begun and the second when it was finished. Sometimes the two dates are only one week apart ("Frantic living", written while having lunch, in a hurry for not getting late for work), some other times a poem is begun but then something happens, whether it is some distraction that doesn't allow me to finish it or a loss of inspiration, or even putting it aside for some reason, keeping it inside a drawer and forgetting about it. Then, one day, I "dig it out" and take it back to life, finding some interest in it and trying to recreate the same mood I had back then and finally finishing it. That is the case of "Declaration of intentions" (nearly four years apart!) and "Transmutation" (six months apart). I *do* hope they ended up becoming something worth reading...

Paulo M. Franco
paulo.m.franco@gmail.com

Testimonials

"Although it is difficult to define poetry, I must confess this is an exciting, readable book that help us to be in touch with the Self embracing the challenges that life presents to us and tests ourselves so often.

These poems are a splendid collection of words, thoughts and sentiments with a solid sense of personality that give us a strong basis for living in this world with feelings, reactions, likes, dislikes, dreams and fears.

Paulo M. Franco's opinion on poetry helps his readers to understand better his writing as he states in his poem "The Notion of Poetry": "… Poetry cannot be prescribed/ Only described/ Felt intensely/ Through the filter of the heart/ And of the soul…""

Maria do Céu Marques, PhD English Philology

"It is said that the eyes are the mirror of the soul, but the words that embrace us as we turn these pages, disclose an inside full of life of an unshakable beauty, supported by a rich and intense experience, a true mirror of the soul. These words are a shout to the Universe, to all human beings, they are the questioning of life, an inventory of feelings, they are Life stripped of itself, the naked universe ready to be molded by each one of us. They are words which make us plunge into ourselves. It encourages us to have an introspective eye, looking for who we really are, on a tireless quest for the true self, framed in all that surrounds us, tangible or not. Words which are stripped from any absurd immodesty, they mainly reveal a will to live. To read and reread."

Manuela Mealha, BA